SandCastle 2

Blends

tr

Carey Molter

Publishing Company

Published by SandCastle™, an imprint of ABDO Publishing Company, 4940 Viking Drive, Edina, Minnesota 55435.

Printed in the United States.

Cover and interior photo credits: Comstock, Corbis Images, Digital Vision, Eyewire Images, PhotoDisc.

Library of Congress Cataloging-in-Publication Data

Molter, Carey, 1973-
      Tr / Carey Molter.
           p. cm. -- (Blends)
      Includes index.
      ISBN 1-57765-411-0
      [1. English language--Phonetics.] I. Title. II. Blends (Series)

      PE1119 .M652 2000
      428.1--dc21

                                                                    00-033203

The SandCastle concept, content, and reading method have been reviewed and approved by a national advisory board including literacy specialists, librarians, elementary school teachers, early childhood education professionals, and parents.

Let Us Know

After reading the book, SandCastle would like you to tell us your stories about reading. What is your favorite page? Was there something hard that you needed help with? Share the ups and downs of learning to read. We want to hear from you! To get posted on the Abdo Publishing Company Web site, send us email at:

sandcastle@abdopub.com

Revised Edition 2002

About SandCastle™
Nonfiction books for the beginning reader

- Basic concepts of phonics are incorporated with integrated language methods of reading instruction. Most words are short, and phrases, letter sounds, and word sounds are repeated.

- Readability is determined by the number of words in each sentence, the number of characters in each word, and word lists based on curriculum frameworks.

- Full-color photography reinforces word meanings and concepts.

- "Words I Can Read" list at the end of each book teaches basic elements of grammar, helps the reader recognize the words in the text, and builds vocabulary.

- Reading levels are indicated by the number of flags on the castle.

Look for more SandCastle books in these three reading levels:

Level 1 (one flag)	**Level 2** (two flags)	**Level 3** (three flags)

Grades Pre-K to K 5 or fewer words per page	**Grades K to 1** 5 to 10 words per page	**Grades 1 to 2** 10 to 15 words per page

tr

Trava tries to make
every day fun.

tr

Travis trusts this puppy.

It will not bite.

tr

Trina and her brother
see something in the
trees.

tr

Trinh likes to walk far.

This trail is truly long.

tr

Trini jumps on the bed.
She might get in
trouble.

tr

Trudy helps Truman
ride his bike.

It has training wheels.

tr

This treat tickles when it trickles down her arm.

tr

It is fun to travel on horses in the country.

tr

What does Patricia
keep her beads on?

(tray)

Words I Can Read

Nouns

A noun is a person, place, or thing

arm (ARM) p. 17
bed (BED) p. 13
bike (BIKE) p. 15
brother (BRUHTH-er)
    p. 9
country (KUHN-tree)
    p. 19
day (DAY) p. 5

fun (FUHN) p. 5
puppy (PUHP-ee) p. 7
trail (TRAYL) p. 11
tray (TRAY) p. 21
treat (TREET) p. 17
trouble (TRUH-buhl)
    p. 13

Plural Nouns

A plural noun is more than one
person, place, or thing

beads (BEEDZ) p. 21
horses (HORSS-ez) p. 19

trees (TREEZ) p. 9
wheels (WEELZ) p. 15

Proper Nouns

A proper noun is the name
of a person, place, or thing

Patricia (puh-TRISH-uh)
    p. 21

Trava (TRAV-uh) p. 5
Travis (TRAV-iss) p. 7

22

Trina (TREEN-uh) p. 9
Trinh (TRIN) p. 11
Trini (TREEN-ee) p. 13

Trudy (TRU-dee) p. 15
Truman (TRU-man)
p. 15

Verbs

A verb is an action or being word

bite (BITE) p. 7
does (DUHZ) p. 21
get (GET) p. 13
has (HAZ) p. 15
helps (HELPSS) p. 15
is (IZ) pp. 11, 19
jump (JUHMP) p. 13
keep (KEEP) p. 21
likes (LIKESS) p. 11
make (MAKE) p. 5
might (MITE) p. 13

ride (RIDE) p. 15
see (SEE) p. 9
tickles (TIK-uhlz) p. 17
travel (TRAV-uhl) p. 19
trickles (TRIK-uhlz)
p. 17
tries (TRYEZ) p. 5
trusts (TRUHSTSS) p. 7
walk (WAWK) p. 11
will (WIL) p. 7

Adjectives

An adjective describes something

every (EV-ree) p. 5
far (FAR) p. 11
fun (FUHN) p. 19
her (HUR) pp. 9, 17, 21
his (HIZ) p. 5

long (LAWNG) p. 11
this (THISS) pp. 7, 11, 17
training (TRANE-ing)
p. 15

23

Match these tr Words to the Pictures

tractor

trash

trumpet

truck

24